BY KATHRYN WALTON

VISIT AMERICA'S NATIONAL PARKS!

VISIT YOSEMITE NATIONAL PARK!

Enslow PUBLISHING

Please visit our website, www.enslow.com. For a free color catalog of all our high-quality books, call toll free 1-800-398-2504 or fax 1-877-980-4454.

Library of Congress Cataloging-in-Publication Data

Names: Walton, Kathryn, 1993- author.
Title: Visit Yosemite National Park! / Kathryn Walton.
Description: Buffalo, NY : Enslow Publishing, [2025] | Series: Visit America's national parks! | Includes index.
Identifiers: LCCN 2024008275 (print) | LCCN 2024008276 (ebook) | ISBN 9781978540699 (library binding) | ISBN 9781978540682 (paperback) | ISBN 9781978540705 (ebook)
Subjects: LCSH: Yosemite National Park (Calif.)–Juvenile literature.
Classification: LCC F868.Y6 W35 2025 (print) | LCC F868.Y6 (ebook) | DDC 979.4/47–dc23/eng/20240220
LC record available at https://lccn.loc.gov/2024008275
LC ebook record available at https://lccn.loc.gov/2024008276

Published in 2025 by
Enslow Publishing
2544 Clinton Street
Buffalo, NY 14224

Portions of this work were originally authored by Frances Nagle and published as *Yosemite National Park*. All new material in this edition is authored by Kathryn Walton.

Designer: Tanya Dellaccio Keeney
Editor: Natalie Humphrey

Photo credits: Series Art (illustration) khezy licious/Shutterstock.com; cover (photo), p. 5 (photo) f11photo/Shutterstock.com; p. 5 (map) Rainer Lesniewski/Shutterstock.com; p. 7 javarman/Shutterstock.com; p. 9 (top) Jeffrey B. Banke/Shutterstock.com; p. 9 (bottom) https://upload.wikimedia.org/wikipedia/commons/a/af/Crown_Mine%2C_Bloody_Canyon_from_Golden_%280bf3d3841be64effb108b80c3ccfe01e%29.jpg; p. 11 https://upload.wikimedia.org/wikipedia/commons/f/fb/Muir_and_Roosevelt_restored.jpg; p. 13 (top) nyker/Shutterstock.com; p. 15 Losonsky/Shutterstock.com; p. 17 Stephen Moehle/Shutterstock.com; p. 17 Gregory B Cuvelier/Shutterstock.com; p. 19 Greg Epperson/Shutterstock.com.

Printed in the United States of America

CPSIA compliance information: Batch #CSENS25: For further information contact Enslow Publishing at 1-800-398-2504.

CONTENTS

WELCOME TO YOSEMITE! 4
COMING THROUGH! 6
CHANGES IN YOSEMITE 8
BECOMING A NATIONAL PARK 10
LIFE IN YOSEMITE 12
SEQUOIA TREES 14
WATERFALLS 16
CLIMBING ROCKS 18
PLANNING YOUR VISIT 20
GLOSSARY 22
FOR MORE INFORMATION 23
INDEX 24

Words in the glossary appear in **bold** type the first time they are used in the text.

WELCOME TO YOSEMITE!

If you take a trip to California, you won't want to miss Yosemite National Park! Around 94 percent of Yosemite National Park is wilderness. Wilderness is land where there are no farms, homes, or other buildings. Yosemite is so wild that you may need a permit to camp in certain places in the park.

Even if you don't want to camp, Yosemite National Park is a great place to hike and explore!

MORE TO KNOW

Over 3 million people visited Yosemite National Park in 2022.

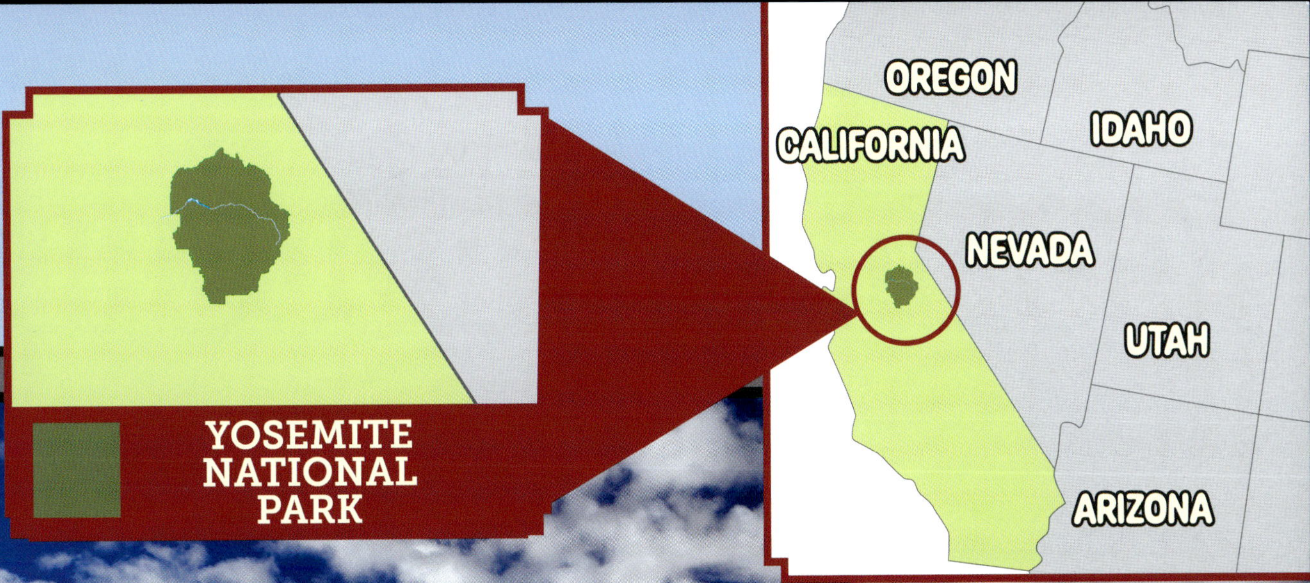

Yosemite is 1,189 square miles (3,080 sq km).

COMING THROUGH!

Millions of years ago, **glaciers** moved through Yosemite National Park. The glaciers formed the rocky cliffs, steep mountains, and other cool **topography** in the park. Much of the rock in the park is granite, and it's very smooth in some places.

Thousands of years ago, more glaciers formed in the Sierra Nevada mountain range. They knocked rocks loose and cut even more of the present **landscape** of the park. The park is still changing today!

If you visit Yosemite, make sure to look out for falling rocks!

MORE TO KNOW

Would you like to see a glacier up close? There still are two glaciers in Yosemite National Park: the Lyell and Maclure glaciers. They may not last much longer.

CHANGES IN YOSEMITE

White settlers didn't set foot in Yosemite until the mid-1800s. Before that, the Ahwahneechee Native Americans lived there, in the valley they called Ahwahnee. This Native American group had lived there for thousands of years. In 1851, soldiers were sent to drive them out.

Some white people who came to the valley were looking for gold. Others wanted to see the valley's beauty in person. But traveling through the mountains was hard. Few people made the trip in the beginning.

MORE TO KNOW

You can't look for gold inside Yosemite National Park. However, there are many places outside the park where you can learn how to look for gold and try finding it yourself!

GOLDEN CROWN MINE

You can still visit what's left of an old gold mining town in Yosemite National Park.

BECOMING A NATIONAL PARK

More white people moved into the valley in the later 1800s, including **photographers** and artists. They hoped to capture the valley's beauty. As more people came to Yosemite Valley, some became worried about harm to the **environment** there. To keep the scenery safe, the government made the area a state park in 1864.

Naturalist John Muir campaigned for the U.S. government to protect more land in the area. In 1890, Congress made Yosemite Valley and the area around it a national park.

MORE TO KNOW

John Muir wrote about Yosemite in a letter to a friend: "It is by far the grandest of all the special temples of nature I was ever permitted to enter."

In 1903, President Teddy Roosevelt (left) camped with John Muir in Yosemite.

LIFE IN YOSEMITE

There are many different **habitats** in Yosemite National Park. This is partly because of the different **elevations** of the Sierra Nevada. There are lakes in the valley and meadows that bloom with wildflowers in the summer. Forests are full of gray foxes, spotted owls, and many kinds of bats.

The higher you go in the park, the fewer plants and animals there are. At the higher elevations though, you can find the Sierra Nevada bighorn sheep!

MORE TO KNOW

The tree line stops at about 9,500 feet (2,896 m). Above that, it's very rocky, cold, and snowy, and trees rarely grow.

Black bears are common in Yosemite National Park.

SEQUOIA TREES

Sequoia (sih-KWOY-uh) trees grow in many places in Yosemite National Park. These giant trees can live to be more than 3,000 years old! The Mariposa Grove alone has about 500 fully grown giant sequoias.

One sequoia, the Grizzly Giant, is more than 2,700 years old and about 100 feet (30 m) around at its base. It's one of the tallest trees in Yosemite at 209 feet (64 m). The tree used to be taller but was struck by lightning.

MORE TO KNOW

The Tuolumne and Merced Groves in Yosemite also have many huge sequoia trees.

The Grizzly Giant was struck by lightning six times during one storm!

WATERFALLS

Yosemite Falls is one of the tallest waterfalls in North America! It is also one of the tallest waterfalls in the world.

It has three parts—the upper falls, the middle cascades, and the lower falls. These parts together add up to 2,425 feet (739 m). Much of Yosemite Falls' volume comes from snow melting high in the mountains. You can just visit the waterfall, or visitors can hike to the top of it!

Horsetail Falls is known for glowing orange during the sunset in February.

MORE TO KNOW

Other waterfalls in the park include Sentinel Falls, which is about 2,000 feet (610 m) high, and Horsetail Falls.

CLIMBING ROCKS

Do you enjoy rock climbing? From the Half Dome to Sentinel Rock, Yosemite has a lot of spots to climb! There are climbs that take just a few hours and those that take days to finish.

There are 800 miles (1,287 km) of hiking trails in the park. One of the most traveled parts of the Pacific Crest National Scenic Trail cuts through Yosemite. This trail starts at the border of Canada and ends at Mexico's border.

MORE TO KNOW

If you want to hike the tallest mountain in Yosemite National Park, look for Mount Lyell! The peak of Mount Lyell is 13,114 feet (3,997 m) high.

If you want to try rock climbing, but don't know where to start, you can visit Yosemite Mountaineering School and Guide Service.

PLANNING YOUR VISIT

Yosemite National Park is a great place to visit at any time during the year. But you may need to plan your trip ahead if you want to go in certain seasons. During the busier times in the park, you will need to make a **reservation** to get inside. You can check what days you need a reservation on Yosemite's website.

No matter when you make the trip to Yosemite, the beauty of this national park can't be beat!

MORE TO KNOW

Winters in Yosemite can be very cold with a lot of **precipitation**. If you visit Yosemite National Park during the winter, make sure to bring a coat.

YOSEMITE NATIONAL PARK

THE FACTS

ESTABLISHED

1919

SIZE

1,189 square miles (3,080 sq km)

NUMBER OF VISITORS EACH YEAR

Over 3 million

NATIVE WILDLIFE

bears, bighorn sheep, western meadowlarks, western pond turtles, and more

NATIVE PLANTS

wildflowers, giant sequoias, hemlock, pines, and more

MUST-SEE STOPS

Yosemite Valley, Yosemite Falls, Pacific Crest National Scenic Trail

GLOSSARY

elevation: Height above sea level.

environment: The natural world in which a plant or animal lives.

glacier: A large area of ice that moves slowly over land.

habitat: The natural place where an animal or plant lives.

landscape: All the features in an area of land that can be seen.

naturalist: Someone who studies plants and animals as they live in nature.

photographer: A person who takes pictures with a camera.

precipitation: Rain, snow, sleet, or hail.

reservation: The act of reserving something, or setting it aside.

topography: The natural and man-made features of a place.

FOR YOUR INFORMATION

Books

Bell, Samantha. *Amazing Heights*. Ann Arbor, MI: Cherry Lake Press, 2024.

Leaf, Christina. *Yosemite National Park*. Minneapolis, MN: Bellwether Media, 2023.

Websites

National Geographic Kids: Yosemite National Park
kids.nationalgeographic.com/nature/article/Yosemite
Learn more about the history of Yosemite National Park.

National Park Service: For Kids
www.nps.gov/yose/learn/kidsyouth/index.htm
Discover more things you can do on your trip to Yosemite.

Publisher's note to educators and parents: Our editors have carefully reviewed these websites to ensure that they are suitable for students. Many websites change frequently, however, and we cannot guarantee that a site's future contents will continue to meet our high standards of quality and educational value. Be advised that students should be closely supervised whenever they access the internet.

INDEX

Ahwahneechee, 8
black bears, 13
California, 4
gold, 8, 9
glaciers, 6, 7
Grizzly Giant, 15
Half Dome, 18
hike, 4, 16, 18
Horsetail Falls, 17
Mariposa Grove, 14
Mount Lyell, 19
Muir, John, 10, 11
Pacific Crest National Scenic Trail, 18, 21
Roosevelt, Teddy, 11
Sentinel Falls, 17
Sentinel Rock, 18
sequoias, 14, 15, 21
Sierra Nevada, 6, 12
size, 5, 21
state park, 10
weather, 20
wildlife, 12, 21
Yosemite Falls, 16, 21